AlC.

To Margaret &

The Wesley C... e
Inspiration

Thank you

Len.

Whilst every effort has been made to provide accurate and factual information at the time of print, the Author and Publishers cannot accept responsibility for any damages suffered as a result of using, modifying, contributing, or copying the information in this guidebook. You have sole responsibility for the implementation of the issues this guidebook raises. In no event shall the Author or Publisher be liable for any indirect, punitive, incidental, or consequential damage (including loss of business, revenue, profits or other economic advantage) however it arises.

CONCISE DIY GUIDEBOOK TO PROJECT MANAGEMENT

A step-by-step guidebook to supervising building projects

For the general public and small businesses

Written by Leonard John Sales ACIOB

Published by
Construction Management Services 99 Ltd
Head Office
Suite 8
Thamesgate Business Centre
Thamesgate House
37 Victoria Avenue
Southend-on-Sea
Essex SS2 6DF

Tel: + 44 (0) 1702 306890 Fax: + 44 (0) 1702 306891

www.project-management-diy.com

First Edition

First published in Great Britain 2003

ISBN 0-9544768-0-8

We run a mail order service, either visit our website or phone for details.

Acknowledgements

Design and layout — Primal Image

Illustrations — Matt Golightly

Cover design — Phil Worman

Section editing — Anthony Watts MBIAT, ACIOB, MaPS

Deborah Ben-Afia
Lynda Sales
Ann Sales

Technical support — The Livemore Partnership.

This guidebook has been enhanced tremendously with the support of TLP. Their common sense and understanding of procedures has helped to convey issues that are usually covered in volumes of complicated jargon.

Proof reading — Yve Bunn B.A. (Hons.)

General thanks to the many people who have supported me during the writing of this guidebook, who are too numerous to mention.

I dedicate this guidebook to the memory of my Mum & Dad

LEN AND PAT SALES

Contents

Appendices

Sample planning programme

Sample specification

Sample programme of works

Sample contract of agreement

Sample method statement

Further reading

Preface

A Project Management Guide Book for the Uninitiated

Many clients cannot understand why they should pay up to 18% of their budget for the services of a building consultant to oversee their project.

Even more so when they may have already paid out approximately 10% of their budget on Architectural fees alongside other professional costs.

Despite the high level of media attention and regular stories of disasters surrounding building projects, most people feel that it will not happen to them and are prepared to risk potential problems, such as poor workmanship, security problems, and projects running over budget and over time.

Although there are many reputable building contractors in the construction industry, there are just as many who are aware that the market is thriving and that most of the domestic work is paid for in cash.

This leads to a situation where some builders are charging extortionate rates for carrying out sub-standard work and getting away with it.

This guidebook is easy to understand and used properly will help to reduce the risk of clients being dissatisfied with their choice of builder and the standard of work.

Most of the elements in this guidebook have had volumes written about them alone. However with this step-by-step approach on the fundamentals, all these elements will become easily manageable, and this will give you confidence in your decision-making.

This guidebook is aimed at clients and individuals who are planning on carrying out small to medium sized projects.

Undertaking a new building project can be a daunting prospect.

By keeping this guidebook simple I have eliminated hours of technical reading, but have still covered the main issues that usually cause problems between builders and clients.

All those who use this guidebook will learn cost saving exercises and how to relay to the professional services and building contractor exactly what is required.

It must be stressed that, as in any form of contract, co-operation and discretion is required from both parties.

About the Author

Leonard Sales ACIOB has been in the construction industry for 26 years from the age of sixteen, and has been responsible for a variety of small, medium, and large projects in the UK and overseas (Middle East).

He had his own building company for ten years, from the age of twenty. He then enrolled in a professional education course, and attended Chelmsford College of Further Education for two and a half years where he qualified for his diploma and certificate in Site Management in July 1992.

This course of sixteen modules was very comprehensive and included Project Finance and Cost Control, Contractual Procedures, Legal Responsibilities, and Health & Safety, leading to a professional qualification.

These qualifications were gained with the Chartered Institute of Building, a world-wide & respected organisation, and in fact enabled him to work on high profile projects in London and the Middle East.

Since the early nineties he has worked in middle and senior management for a variety of companies and has been involved in many different styles of management.

He has learnt from this experience that clients who demand the highest standards and are willing to work in conjunction with the contractor, are the ones who generally get their projects finished on time and to budget.

He has observed that Architects generally do not want to get involved in overseeing the smaller projects as this is too time-consuming for them, and in most cases would be too expensive for the domestic client.

It is with this in mind that he has written this guidebook for the general public and small businesses, and when used with common sense and confidence it can assist in the smooth running of all types of projects.

Included in this guidebook are simple-to-use management techniques that he has used successfully, that would suit projects with values ranging from £1k to £1million.

Introduction

A growing number of clients have been disappointed with the standard of work and additional time taken on their building projects, which inevitably lead to additional costs.

This guidebook has been written to raise awareness of the pitfalls to avoid, the regulations to be met, and the best way to monitor works from start to finish.

I have tried to cover many of the critical areas related to Project Management in as few words as possible, to avoid long and complicated contractual jargon. It must be stressed that each project is unique and some will require more planning than others.

Some projects will only require implementation of a few elements of this guidebook whereas others may require much more.

You may feel that you want a more legally binding contract, which your Architect or Legal representative should be able to organise for you.

It would be fair to say that if you tried to implement all of the procedures in this guidebook on one single project, the builder would probably run a mile.

You need to study this guidebook from start to finish and pick out the elements that are suitable for the size of project that you are undertaking, and which you feel comfortable in implementing.

Do remember that it is your money that is being spent, so you need to be in control at all times and confident in your decision-making.

Set out a plan of action, study it and make changes where necessary until you are satisfied that you have covered all aspects. This does not mean to say that you need a procedure or complicated paperwork exercise for each element, only that you have at least thought about and discussed the issues.

Most of the methods in this guidebook can be scaled down if required and used on projects from about £1,000 upwards.

If you feel that you are unable to Project Manage your own building work, do consider using a consultant, who should be able to make the necessary cost savings to cover at least some of their fees, depending on the size of the project.

Do remember that this is a guidebook and some builders may fulfil the criteria for appearing professional but may not perform when required.

Monitoring, inspecting and good communication will keep you well informed of any problems that may arise.

Getting Started

Before starting on any kind of building work to your home or business, you need to know exactly what you need, and what you are hoping to achieve.

You also need to decide whether or not your ideas are practical and know that you have the financial resources to carry them out.

Once you are satisfied that your ideas are feasible, you need to decide on your budget.

It is important to understand that any decisions that you make now can have serious cost implications later on.

If you have little or no knowledge at all of what is practical, you will need to contact an Architect or specialist designer, depending on your requirements.

This may cost up to £80.00 per hour or a fixed fee of the percentage of the project; however if you do not start off on the right track it could cost you much more in the long run.

If an Architect carries out work on your behalf on an agreed percentage of the project and for some reason the project does not proceed, his fee may be payable on an hourly rate of £80.00ph which would soon mount up to a considerable sum for a full set of working drawings.

Architects, Engineers and Designers will know what is required to obtain Planning Permission (if needed) and Building Regulation approval.

It is worth obtaining quotes from professionals before engaging in any form of contract as their charges can vary drastically depending on their workload.

Architects and Designers are market-led and in boom times may have six months' work booked in advance, therefore they will have the upper hand when negotiating fees, so be patient and shop around.

You can minimize the initial costs by putting together as much information as possible. This will cut down on the amount of time they would normally spend in extracting your ideas from you.

It is easy enough to explain to someone what you want but as the saying goes, "a picture paints a thousand words".

Basic sketches can help to avoid misunderstandings and will help to avoid re-drawing and costs for abortive works.

This will also help to speed the whole process up, as some professionals will use the design element as a tool for taking time to provide drawings, particularly if they have a heavy workload.

Remember, conception to on-site development can take more time than the building process itself.

It is advisable to draw up a timetable of things to be done which will help you to keep track of the dates for issuing information etc. (see sample planning programme).

It should be noted that all professional consultants are required by their governing body to carry professional indemnity insurance to cover any claims made against them for failures in their services/designs.

Non-qualified designers (one man bands) may be less expensive, but may not always be competent and could prove difficult or impossible to recover money from if sued!

As far as professional fees are concerned, you should look at paying around 5% -15% of your budget (construction costs) depending on the complexity and value of the project.

Planning Permission & Scheme Design

- Once you have decided on what you require, your Architect or Designer will produce drawings based on your ideas, which should take into account the planning authority's criteria.

- Most projects will require planning permission although minor domestic works such as porches, conservatories etc may be approved as "Permitted Development" (not requiring a planning application) by the local authority. But this should always be checked with them as the rules are complex, and it is always sensible to obtain written confirmation if this is the case.

- Whilst the local authority has planning guidelines (local plan) these are open to interpretation and, even if the planning officer is in favour of the scheme, it can often be refused by the planning committee.

- Planning permission has to be obtained for most major building works and this deals with the issues surrounding the design e.g. use and appearance (plans & elevation) - which should not be confused with the construction drawings e.g. sections, details etc.

- The Planning Authority will consider the impact that the development will have on the site and surrounding area. Not only will they consult with adjoining neighbours but they may also obtain advice/consent from other departments such as Highways, Environmental Health or other organisations such as English Heritage.

- Part of the planning process involves notifying/advertising the development, and the basic details can be found in the local press or the "yellow" site notice displayed on the site boundary.

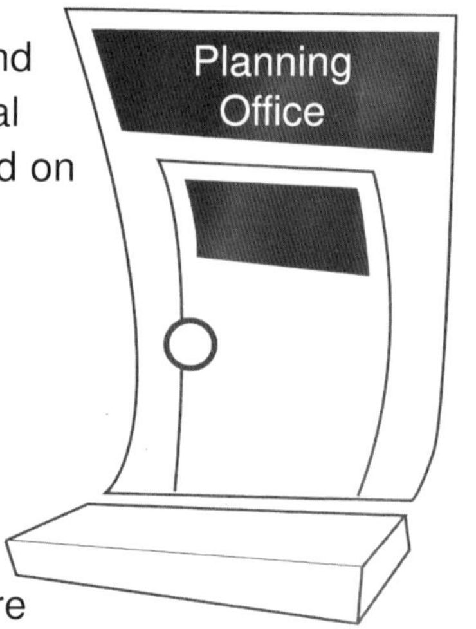

- This allows interested parties 21 days to inspect the deposited plans and make comments to the planning departments. Obtaining planning consent can be a lengthy process and will take at least 6—8 weeks although in practice it is more like 12—16 weeks on simple projects.

- It is a legal requirement to obtain planning consent (if needed) and works started without planning approval can be stopped by an injunction from the Local Authority, which may also incur fines.

- Normally planning permission (consent) lasts for 5 years (5 years in which to start the work).

Building Regulations

- The Building Regulations are completely different from Local Authority Planning Approval and are concerned with the construction of the building and its services.

- They evolved following the Great Fire of London and were used to protect the public from dangerous building construction, and improve public hygiene, e.g. foul drainage etc.

- The Building Regulations continued to expand and now cover most areas of construction.

- The "Building Regulations" is a legal document and is divided into the following sections giving minimum standards of design and construction:

  A: Structure
  B: Fire Safety
  C: Site Preparation and Resistance to Moisture
  D: Toxic Substances
  E: Resistance to the Passage of Sound
  F: Ventilation
  G: Hygiene
  H: Drainage and Waste Disposal
  J: Heat-producing Appliances
  K: Stairs, Ramps and Guards
  L: Conservation of Fuel and Power
  M: Access and Facilities for Disabled People
  N: Glazing – Materials and Protection

- The Building Regulations continue to grow in size and complexity. New areas being considered are Electrical Installations and the use of recycled building materials/products (conservation of natural resources).

- Your Architect will know which regulations are required for your project and will incorporate them in the drawings both in writing and where necessary in detailed drawings.

- These "regs" are inspected by BCOs (Building Control Officers) who ensure the plans that have been approved are being followed.

- It is the responsibility of the builder to inform the BCO when each of these regulations needs to be inspected.

- Elements that need to be inspected at various stages differ but they include:

  - ♦Excavations
  - ♦Foundations
  - ♦Membranes (damp proof courses etc)
  - ♦Drainage
  - ♦Structural elements etc

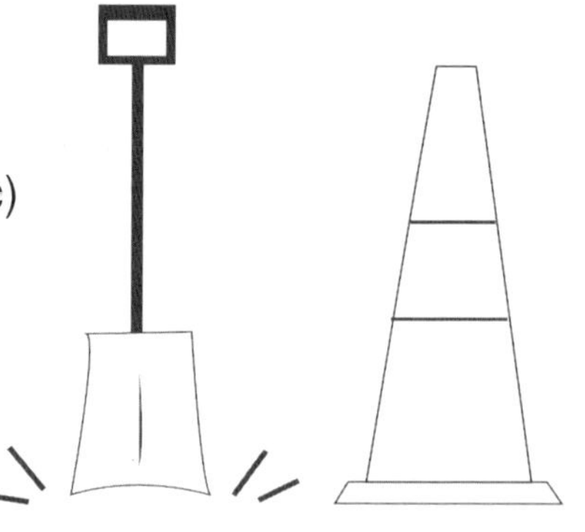

- Whilst the works are inspected by the BCO it should be noted that they cannot be held responsible for defective work as the responsibility lies with the designer or builder.

- Although the BCO must be invited to inspect the work at various stages they have no obligation to do so.

- Within the domestic side of the construction industry there are five main categories of works that may require Planning Permission and Building Regulations consent (approval):

  - ♦ Extensions
  - ♦ Loft Conversions
  - ♦ Garages
  - ♦ Major Internal Alterations
  - ♦ Major External Work

- **Note:** even replacement windows are covered by the Building Regulations although some window manufacturers/suppliers are licensed to undertake these works without the need for a formal application to the Local Authority.

- Alterations to the building structure or services require Building Regulation Approval, although small building works can often be carried out using a "Building Notice" application requiring limited information or plans. Often the Building Inspector will just visit the site to discuss and inspect the works.

Extensions

- To have an extension built you will require scaled drawings, which will need to be drawn up by an Architect or similar qualified person.

- You will need to apply for planning permission and have the approval of your local planning authority.

- The local planning office can be contacted via your Borough Council Offices.

- Having drawings prepared and approved can be a long drawn-out affair so be mindful of this from the outset.

- From conception of projects to actually starting work can vary from 6 weeks to 6 months depending on the size and nature of the project.

- In some cases, such as in listed buildings, this may be longer and could even be rejected for numerous reasons.

Loft Conversions

- Again loft conversions will require scaled drawings, which will need to meet current building regulations.

- You may find that there are differences in dimensions between the drawings and the finished project; this is because it is sometimes difficult to survey lofts and existing structures accurately, where access is difficult or dangerous.

- Never have loft conversions or extensions built without contacting your local authority as this work will be picked up in any surveys that are carried out when selling your property, and may cause you problems.

Garages

- You will require drawings and may need planning approval, but in most cases this is a more straightforward affair, depending on the location and size in relation to the main building.

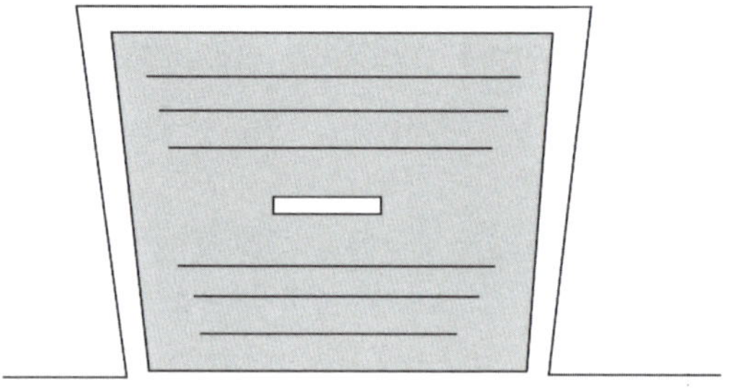

Internal Alterations

- These do not necessarily require planning approval but for your own peace of mind it is worth enquiring with your local authority.

- One cautionary note is that when you are planning to have two rooms knocked into one, for example, a structural engineer would be required to ensure that the correct size supports are introduced, if needed.

External works

- There are certain regulations regarding garden walls and fencing; your Local Authority will advise you of these. With external works you do not neccessarily need precise drawings, however a good sketch of your requirements will help to avoid misunderstandings.

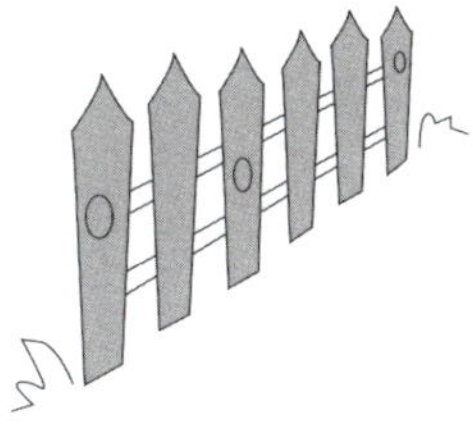

Trees

- If you are planning to have trees removed, you must first ensure that they do not have a TPO (tree protection order) against them. Your Local Authority will advise you on this. Beware of cutting down trees that are very close to buildings as this is a major cause of subsidence.

- Cutting down trees with TPOs is an offence for which you can be fined.

- Most of the above works will include Mechanical or Electrical elements.

Mechanical & Electrical

- Mechanical and Electrical as it is known in the construction industry covers all works associated with the main services.

- Mechanical: Plumbing & Heating
  Ventilation
  Drainage
  Irrigation
  Gas appliances

- Electrical: Lighting and Power
  Security Alarms
  Audio
  Phones
  Cable TV

- Fully qualified Technicians should carry out and certify all of the above elements of work, whether or not they are working for a builder.

- You may have to organise some of these independently of works being undertaken by a builder, particularly the utilities and communication companies.

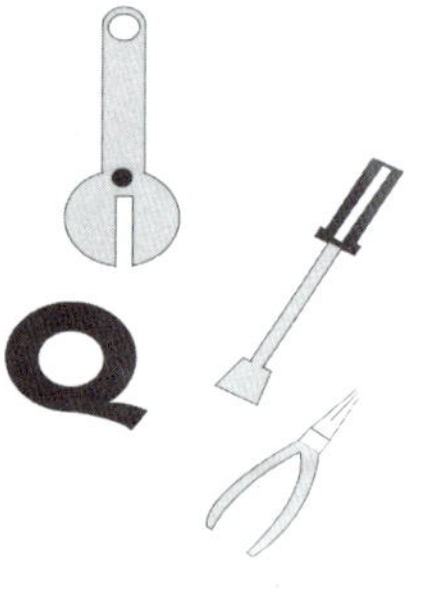

Legal Requirements

- Apart from Statutory Legal Requirements and insurance policies needed to start a business, individual projects may need insurance cover for the building works.

- As a rule of thumb insurance for the building works and material etc in new buildings is the responsibility of the contractor.

- Works to existing buildings are normally covered by the client's insurance, and it is necessary for them to ensure that they notify their building insurance company prior to any work commencing. Failure to notify insurance companies may invalidate any future claim or cover (always confirm in writing or get proof of insurance).

- It should never be presumed that Planning and Building Regulations Approval is all that is required by the builder or the client.

Note: A building lease or deeds may have restrictions, and the freeholder or owner may need to give consent. If in doubt consult a solicitor.

Condition Schedule

- In order to protect the client's/contractor's interest, a condition schedule should be written up. This would be a record of the areas surrounding the works in case there is any dispute later about damage caused during the works.

- A condition schedule may take the form of photographs or agreed lists of defects or damages that are apparent prior to the work starting.

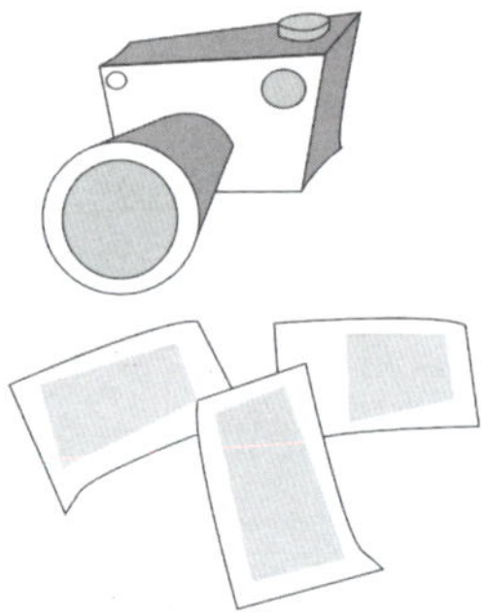

- Without this agreed condition schedule the contractor may face claims for damages or be asked to repair or redecorate parts of the building or site previously damaged by others.

- This should be extended to cover adjoining buildings, to protect the client from claims by neighbours.

Party Wall Awards

- Any building works close to or adjoining another property may require a "party wall award" to be agreed between the client and his neighbour.

- A professional party wall surveyor can undertake this service, and may well need to be consulted at an early stage, as this is a legal requirement that could hold up or stop the work progressing if agreements have not been approved prior to construction.

- Needless to say this could have a severe financial implication on commercial building projects.

Know Your Requirements

Specification

- The specification of your project has to be a detailed description of the materials that will be used, and written in such a way that there is no room for misunderstandings.

- Most cost increases arise from changes to design and specifications and/or clarification of inadequate specification.

- It is important that you list all of the elements that you know will form each part of the works, and then break these elements down to ensure that they will meet your expectations of the finished product.

- The specification will be included either on the drawing or as a separate document. I have included a sample specification in the appendix.

- There are regulations that govern some of the materials that will be used such as underground drainage.

- There are cost savings that can be made by using alternative materials. This is something that you will need to discuss with your builder or material supplier.

- If you notice material changes from that in the specification, speak to your builder about this as he may be making cost savings at your expense!

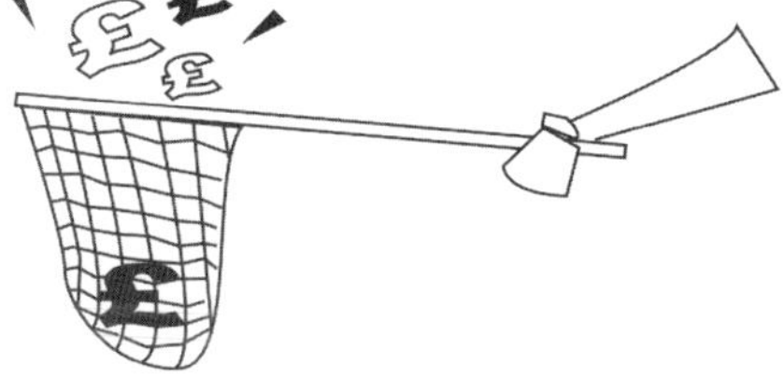

- When it comes to the finishes you must ensure that it is **your** specification that is being worked to, and that they are specific to **your** requirements.

- Your local building material supplier and associated suppliers will normally be happy to assist in advising on the appropriate materials for given situations; do not be afraid to ask.

- It is worth taking the time to cover as much as possible in the specification as this will be an important factor when obtaining quotes.

- The more detailed information you can provide will enable the contractor to price on a “like for like” basis which allows you to judge fairly between quotations.

- All building works including plumbing, heating, and electrical must meet certain regulations, which will require certification.

Security

- This is an area that does not usually have enough attention paid to it by builders in general, yet it is one that can cause the biggest problems.

- When you employ the services of a builder or contractor you would naturally assume that he has thought about security and weather protection.

- This is not always the case and when things go wrong in this department it can sour relations severely.

- If there is any doubt about the security that is being provided, most insurance companies will use this to avoid making payment on claims for theft or damage.

- Most building work will entail the need for workers to have access to parts of the main building on a regular basis.

- You must take all precautions to avoid any unforeseen problems. This is explained in chapter 6 under Method Statements.

Health & Safety

- There are particular Health & Safety Regulations for the construction industry, which are very comprehensive.
- Your builder should be aware of these regulations; however the domestic side of the construction industry is not regulated to the extent that it should be.
- Domestic builders are starting to understand that they have a responsibility to you as a client, and their own employees, with regard to Health & Safety.
- Do not be afraid to ask a potential builder for his safety policy.
- If he readily agrees to this and you find yourself with the document within a day or two, the chances are he has a professional approach to his work.
- If however he does not know what you are talking about, it does not mean that he is not capable of carrying out his work safely.

- It is important to let him know that you expect consideration in this respect, and that you would like to see some evidence that he is meeting his health & safety obligations.

- If you get nothing at all from him it is unlikely that he takes the issue seriously.

- It is worth visiting property which is currently being worked on by any builders that you may be considering using, before engaging in any contract. This will enable you to see how he operates, the cleanliness of the site etc.

A clean site is generally a safe site.

Contacting Contractors

Size of Project

- It is important to know that individual contractors are capable of undertaking projects within their experience, capability and financial scope.

- This is an important factor with cash-flow on the larger projects, as the contractor will be expected to finance the initial stages. He can expect to receive payments in arrears by up to two months on the larger projects!

- You must make any potential contractor aware of your estimated budget, and that you will be making stage payments, which is covered in chapter 7.

Directories

- One place to start is the telephone directory such as the Yellow Pages; this is particularly useful as the more professional builder will normally belong to one of the major trade associations and will show their logo on the advert.

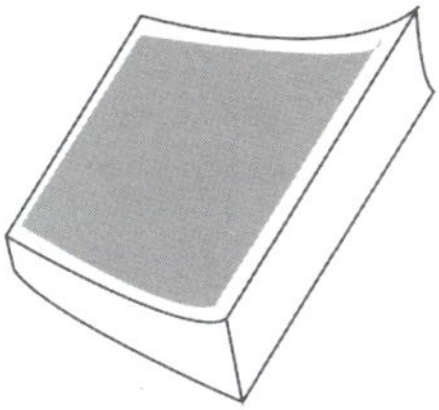

- This does not mean to say that they are better, just that they are prepared to have information about themselves available to a third party.

Local Papers

- Small one-man operation builders generally advertise in this way and service the smaller projects.

Recommendation

- Most people know someone who has had work carried out and this is probably one of the most reassuring ways of finding a reliable builder, as you can find out first-hand if there were any problems.

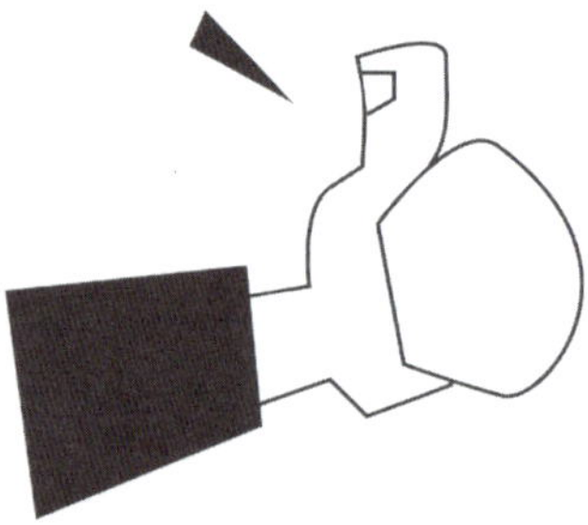

- This may even give you the opportunity of inspecting the work that they carried out to see the quality of workmanship.

- You may know someone who is having work done; you will get no better feel for a company than actually seeing how they operate and how the men treat the client's premises!!!

Advertising Boards

- As you travel around you will see many signs of work being carried out. Take a good look at the cleanliness of the site and note whether the area is tidy.

- Builders who are prepared to put a board outside a job or who advertise on their vans are in the main confident in their wo' .

Internet

- If you have access to the internet you can find local builders who may even have their own website.
- This will allow you to find out much more about how they operate in advance of contacting them.
- Remember that builders generally have to plan their work well in advance and may have order books as long as six months or more.

Response

- Depending on market forces, you may find that you get an initial favourable response; however it is a fact that with other work commitments many contractors do not respond as quickly as clients would like.
- In many cases they may not respond at all if it is a project that they are not particularly interested in.
- A contractor will not necessarily tell you that he is not interested so it is worth seeking six or seven quotes from which you may get three who respond.
- Do not wait to see what response you get; be prepared to chase the quote.

Establishing Credibilty

Reference Checks

- Whichever method you have used to find a contractor it is advisable to satisfy yourself that he is capable of carrying out the works to the standards that you expect.

- If the contractor has not come via recommendation, ask him if he has any objection to showing you projects of a similar size which he has carried out.

- Do not be afraid to ask for written references from satisfied cus tomers who you may wish to contact for confirmation.

• There are agencies that you can contact to carry out credit checks, which you may decide to use if you feel that your chosen builder may not be in a position to finance the initial stages of the project.

• I must point out that if a project did get into difficulties and the builder was unable to complete the project, the next builder would be justified in charging more than the going rate to take over.

Portfolio

• Contractors with a comprehensive photographic portfolio are generally client orientated and only too willing to help with design input to finishes.

Company Set-up

- It is worth taking the time and effort to visit the prospective contractor's office set-up as this will give you some idea of his professionalism.

- You could ask the contractor if you can visit a project that he is currently working on. This will also give you an insight into the level of client orientation and on site cleanliness/conditions.

- You will find that by taking the time to carry out these checks, you will get an understanding of the contractor's capabilities which will dictate whether you proceed with obtaining a quote.

Insurance

- Most reputable contractors will have adequate insurance; however it is important that you contact your own insurance company to ascertain the necessary requirements.

- Your own insurance may be invalidated if you do not inform your insurance company of any building works being undertaken, particularly where scaffolding or excavations are involved.

- Your insurance company may ask you to provide copies of the relevant policies held by the contractor.

- It is advisable not to allow any building work to be carried out by uninsured builders/contractors.

Obtaining and Agreeing Quotes

Like-for-Like Quotes

- In order for you to compare competitive quotes, the contractors must be given the same information.

- This can only be achieved by the specification (as described in chapter two), and any drawings that have been prepared.

- Some projects may require the contractors to carry out their own measurements and inspections which may bring to light elements that have not been included in the specification.

- If they do pick up elements that have not been detailed, ensure that these form part of the written quote.

Break-down of Quote

- Do not be afraid to ask the contractor to give you a break-down of his quote, as this is a good way of removing some elements of the contract to make cost savings.

- As you will see in the sample programme of work, the work is broken down into various elements in order to measure productivity against expenditure.

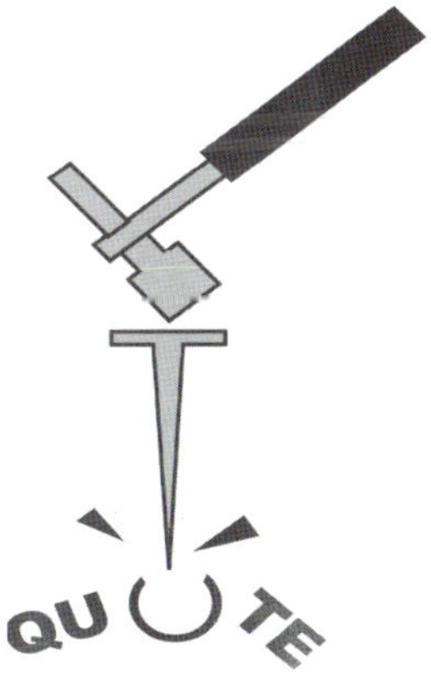

- You can use the individual elements of the program of works to form the break-down of the quote.

Cost-Saving Exercises

- Once all of your information has been collated and quotes are obtained you will know the real figures involved in your project.
- You may well be surprised and have some money left from your original budget.
- Do not be tempted to make rash decisions at this point, as you should always have a contingency sum to cover any unforeseen problems that may occur.
- If however your budget costs are exceeded by say 15% do not be alarmed, as there are many ways to make cost savings without compromising the quality of workmanship or materials.
- Builders will mainly use sub-contractors for the specialist work and as such they will have a pretty high mark-up on elements such as ceramic tiling and laminated floor finishes.
- By eliminating these from the contract you may be able to get alternative quotes at a later date from local suppliers (after the builder has completed his work) which may be as much as 30% lower than that quoted in the builder's estimate.

- The only downfall of removing elements from the builder's package is that the work tends to drag on, so it is worth weighing up what is more important to you when making these decisions.

Examples of Cost Savings

- ♦ Carrying out your own decoration
- ♦ Supplying your own sanitary ware
- ♦ Supplying your own carpets and soft furnishings
- ♦ Reducing the extent of external work to ensure the main works are complete
- ♦ Removing elements of work such as cornices, dado rails, ceramic tiling, mirrors etc.

- Reducing the specification, e.g.

  - ♦ Smaller skirting
  - ♦ Less expensive ironmongery and fittings
  - ♦ Less expensive light fittings etc.

- As you can see there are many ways in which to make cost savings, you just need to examine your specification and prioritise accordingly.

Timescale Programme

- When inviting contractors to quote, ensure that they include a programme of work to show how long they anticipate working on your project.

- You have to make a comparison against the amount of time that you will be inconvenienced against the difference in quotes, for example one contractor may quote £21k for a two storey extension that he estimates will take six weeks against another who quotes £20k but estimates a timescale of ten weeks.

- These are important issues that need serious consideration and discussion, as relations between client and contractor can quickly deteriorate when projects are not completed on time and to budget.

Extras-Variations

- This is a very important area for discussion and is one that can cause a problem between client and contractor if the specification is not comprehensive.

- You must endeavour to avoid extras or variations being carried out without your authorisation.

- It is inevitable that there will be some extras or variations.

- What you must discuss and agree on is whether this work will be carried out on an hourly or priced basis.

- You must discuss any extras or variations with the person with whom you placed the contract, and not anyone working for him, although this can sometimes be unavoidable.

- Write down all extras or variations and remember that some of these variations may involve cost savings.

- If you do make changes to the scope of works, obtain a quotation or estimate for the new works before agreeing for the work to proceed.

- Remember, once the contractor has been awarded the main contract his prices may not be as keen with no competition.

- Bear in mind though, that if a contractor has to bring in outside assistance above that which has been planned, he may have to pay over the normal going rate.

- This is sometimes worth the additional cost if it means that the project is on schedule.

Starting the Work

Contract of Agreement

- Some contractors may ask you to enter into a contract with them, which would generally indicate a professional set-up; however the domestic sector does not usually have such safeguards.

- The advantage of entering into a contract especially when large sums of money are involved is that you have a legal document, which relates to the written quote from the contractor.

- The contract should include terms of payment, and any bonus/incentive clause as explained in chapter 7.

- Included in this guidebook is a sample contract of agreement which will give you an idea of what you need to cover.

- You may decide to write your own contract but we do advise you to seek legal advice if you are in any doubt.

- Always have any financial agreement confirmed in writing.

- A formal contract of agreement is meant to protect the interest of both parties, so if the contractor refuses to enter into such an agreement it may be best to choose one that does.

- Formal contracts do not have to be sanctioned by a solicitor but it is advisable to have a third party witness the agreement.

- Alternatively "off the shelf" contracts are available such as JCT (Joint Contracts Tribunal) Home owners/occupiers.

The JCT Building Contract covers the following areas;

Part 1 The arrangements for the work

A The work to be done
B Planning permission, building regulations and party walls
C Using facilities on the premises
D Price
E Payment
F The working period
G Product guarantees
H Insurances
I Working hours
J Occupation and security of the premises
K Disputes

Part 2 The conditions

1 Carrying out the work-contractor's responsibilities
2 Carrying out the work-customer's responsibilities
3 Health and Safety
4 Changing the work details
5 Extending the working period
6 Payment
7 Contractor's continuing responsibility for faults in the work
8 Bringing the contract to an end, by either party
9 Insolvency
10 Other rights and remedies
11 Law of contract

Method Statement

What is a method statement?

- This is not a term that the general public will always be familiar with, and in fact most domestic builders will not have been required to produce one.

- A Method Statement is a descriptive account of the method in which a particular operation will be carried out (how the builder will carry out the work, or what precautions he will be taking to ensure security of your property).

- It is not unreasonable for you to request one for certain elements of the work such as any work that may cause a security risk or safety issue, or where the sequence of work is important to minimise inconvenience.

- A contractor may put up resistance in providing method statements; however he only needs to discuss these elements with you, and this should be recorded.

- You may be required to produce the information for your insurance company.

Inspection Procedure

- It is very important to establish an inspection procedure of all works on a regular basis and to ensure that you inform the contractor in writing of anything that is giving you cause for concern.

- It is always advisable to inspect the works as items progress or finish. Not only will this give the contractor the impression that you are taking an active interest in the quality of the work, but it will provide an opportunity to discuss and correct items before it's too late.

- Contractors rely on sub-contractors and sometimes have difficulty in getting them to site when required, particularly in times of boom.

- Let the main contractor's staff know if there is a problem before they leave site, as it may be difficult to get them back to site to rectify any defects once they have started another contract elsewhere.

- Always put your concerns in writing and remember to inform the main contractor as the first point of contact.

Financial Arrangement

Valuations

- If you are financing the project yourself, do not pay money up front if you can help it, as you need to maintain control at all times.

- We mentioned in chapter 6 that terms of payment should be agreed in the contract or at the very least confirmed in writing.

- A mortgage company may finance a project under the conditions that payments are made on completion of certain stages.

- These stages are the basis on which the valuations are made which includes the amount of work and material that has been put into the project.

- You need to be certain that the contractor understands these requirements and is prepared to finance the project up to these stages.

- It is advisable to have a contingency plan in place to cover any unforeseen financial circumstances.

Payments

- Once the valuation has been agreed, based on the amount of work that has been carried out and assuming standards are satisfactory, payment can be made.

- It is advisable to have an agreement to pay within seven days so that the contractor will have carried out a further week's work rather than be paid up to date.

- This is merely a safeguard. Always get a signed receipt for any money that is paid out.

- Final Payment: Apart from the building works being complete, ensure you have all test certificates and warranties in place before you make final payment.

- Items such as central heating or new boilers require certification before they are handed over as complete.

- When Building Regulation Applications are made, the client can request a `completion certificate` from the Building Inspector to certify that the main works are completed to his specification.

- Often this is required by lending institutions. Ensure that the contractor provides this before all the money is released to him.

Bonus/Incentive

- This is a scheme that could be put in place where a client stands to lose out financially if the project overruns.

- With mutual agreement you could introduce an incentive bonus arrangement based on the project being completed on or within the agreed time.

- The bonus would be worked out on the number of weeks or days under the agreed period.

- Two things to be mindful of if entering into such a scheme are that any additional work can affect the finishing date and that your specification needs to be comprehensive.

- The likelihood of the project being complete way ahead of schedule is slim, whereas projects running over are common.

Operation & Maintenance Manuals

Operation Manuals

- With all new installations whether they are mechanical, electrical or other, such as windows, doors etc, there are always operating instructions.

- You must ensure that the contractor hands these over to you, and where necessary arranges a demonstration.

Maintenance Manuals

- Again all new installations should be accompanied by maintenance manuals.
- It is vital that these are read and understood as any guarantee may be affected if they are not complied with.

Test Certificates

- During the course of the works there are certain elements that require tests to be carried out and certified. It is advisable to ask the contractor for copies of such tests to add to your documents.

Guarantees

- As with most guarantees they do not come into effect until such time as they are registered.
- This is one element that is regularly overlooked.
- Ensure that all manufacturers' guarantees are handed over at the end of the project.

Guarantees that should be handed over include:

- Central heating equipment and plumbing fittings
- Electrical installation equipment and fittings
- UPVC or Aluminium windows and doors
- Appliances
- Damp proof injection

- Waterproof rendering
- Specialist flat roof systems
- Velux windows
- Door furniture
- Specialist works e.g. laminate flooring

Good Working Relations

Meetings

- Establish from the very start of the project a regular timeframe for meetings with a senior member of the contractor's team, or the contractor himself.

- It is important that you are informed of progress on a regular basis to avoid any surprises.

- Your meeting agenda should include:
    - ♦ Progress against Programme
    - ♦ Delays
    - ♦ Extras-Variations
    - ♦ Inspections
    - ♦ Health and Safety issues

Written Correspondence

- You will have learnt from this guidebook that written evidence of quotes, specifications, contracts etc is very important.

- Any professional contractor will be only too happy to receive and send written confirmation of verbal agreements.

- If you enter into any form of contract with only verbal agreements you are leaving yourself wide open in the event of anything going wrong.

Avoid Conflict

- The construction industry by its very nature is one that causes inconvenience to the client and possibly to neighbours and the general public.

- It can be very frustrating to have dust and noise for weeks on end. It is advisable to inform neighbours of your intentions so that they can make allowances.

- Your contractor should furnish you with enough information about how he intends running the project for there not to be any nasty surprises.

- In any eventuality it is important to maintain good working relations and confirm any concerns that you may have in writing, rather than getting into conflict.

Photographic Records

- It is advisable to take plenty of photographs of the work as it proceeds. Apart from the opportunity of looking back and seeing how your property has changed it would be crucial evidence in the case of things going disastrously wrong.

- Some contractors feel uncomfortable when clients take photos, but this is easily remedied by telling them that you are taking them to show your friends the changes - and that they may be used for his portfolio once the project is satisfactorily completed.

- If you have any reservations about any aspect of the work either before or during the contract you must bring this to the contractor's attention straight away.

Record Keeping

Drawing Issue

- From the very outset of any building or home improvement project, you should have produced sketches or scaled drawings.

- Whether you have produced your own drawings or had them drawn up by a professional it is very important to keep a simple drawing register.

- Whenever you issue any sketches or drawings they should be dated and given a number.

- If any changes are made they should be marked as superseded and the new drawing should be dated and given a revision code which would normally start with A, and any further revisions would continue with alphabetical revision codes.

- You must always ensure that the builder is working to the current drawings. Late changes or outdated information will add to the project cost and may extend the programme.

Project File

- It is worth starting a project file with separate sections for the different elements involved.

- It would not be unusual to have up to 11 sections where you can easily access the information.

  - Example:
    - Architect
    - Engineer
    - Contract drawings/documents
    - Building contractor
    - Local Authority
    - Contract documents
    - Utilities companies
    - O & M Manuals
    - Insurance details
    - Payment details
    - Miscellaneous

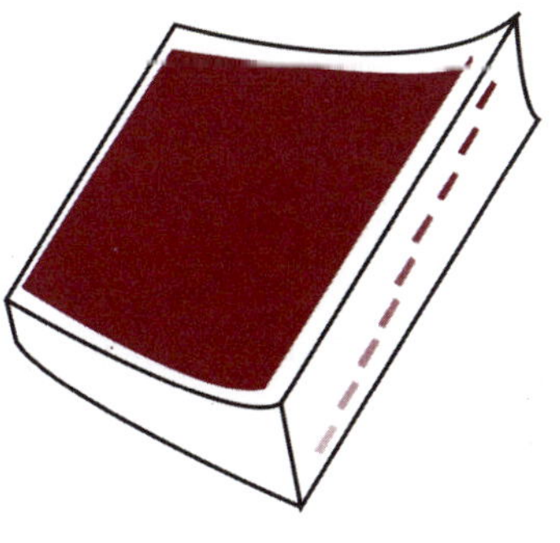

Diary

- It is very important to keep a diary of all telephone calls and a brief description of what was discussed, any action that you have been asked to carry out, and confirmation of any agreements that have been made.

- If you change the specification for any reason, make sure that you confirm to the contractor, in writing, the details of those changes.

- Any changes that are made may have financial implications and you will need to know either way what these costs are.

- Contractors do not particularly like to reduce the cost of the work, even if the amount of work has been reduced.

- You should also record an account of the work carried out each day, the labour on site each day and any problems that may have occurred.

- It is advisable to keep a record of the weather and any additional work that has been carried out as this may affect the completion date.

Telephone numbers

- During the course of any project you will inevitably gather many telephone numbers related to the project, which can be entered in a single page in your diary under five categories.

♦ Professional Team: Architect, Engineer, BCO
♦ Building Contractor (include emergency numbers for out of hours)
♦ Services: Gas, Electric, Telephone, Water
♦ Emergency Numbers
♦ Suppliers

- It is important that the builder issues you with the telephone numbers of his contractors in the event that you are unable to contact him, subject to the type of work being carried out.

- These would normally include:

♦ Scaffold company
♦ Roofer
♦ Electrician
♦ Plumber
♦ Glazier

Professional and Site Teams

The Construction Team

- Construction companies are usually categorised as Large, Medium, and Small.

- Since this guidebook is aimed mainly at the domestic market we will not go into detail about the different roles of the professional departments within a large construction company. However this organisation chart will give you an example of a small company's management structure.

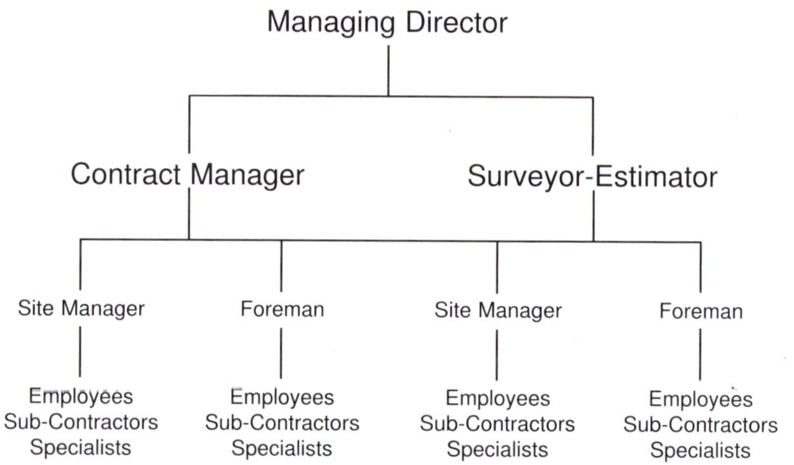

Site Manager

- Site Managers do not usually carry out any practical work and are normally detailed to projects which require close co-ordination of sub-contractors and precise continuity of material. These projects would normally be in the range of £200k and upwards.

- It is the Site Manager's duty to ensure that the day-to-day running of the site is carried out to meet the regulations that are laid down by the construction industry regulatory bodies.

- He must ensure that site personnel are adequately trained and competent for the tasks which they are being asked to carry out.

- Site Managers are usually given the responsibility to make decisions which directly affect the site and the well-being of all personnel affected by it. This would include the client, visitors (whether invited or not) and the immediate neighbours, among many others.

- If the Site Manager is unable to satisfy your requirements for any reason it is at this point that you contact his superior. This could be the Contract Manager or Director of the company.

- If the project does not warrant a full time Site Manager, there must be an appointed person who is responsible for the site activities and Health & Safety requirements, such as First Aid.

Foreman

- The site foreman would normally carry out practical work but would also be expected to make decisions affecting the work and would co-ordinate the operations on site, including ordering of material etc.

- The foreman would usually be instructed by his head office in matters of the specification of work, and as such would not be expected to act on information from the client unless he had been given the training and responsibility to record and communicate any changes or revisions to the specification.

Sub-contractor and Specialists

- The sub-contractor would normally be on a fixed price to the builder for his specific area of work, e.g. roof tiling, ceramic tiling, heating etc.

- Sub-contractors will not usually carry out any changes to the specification which affects their work, without prior instruction from the main contractor.

- Always remember that if you change the specification on site it will affect the eventual cost of the project. Be sure that you know the consequences of changes before you make them (where possible).

- Changes to the specification can sometimes be incorporated in the original quote. However where there is a material change, costs may be incurred due to the duration of the project being extended even if the material is the same price. Re-stocking of material and revised delivery times come at a price.

Suppliers

- The main contractor would normally supply and install the main building material as this is a major part of the continuity of any project.

- Where you the client are supplying material such as kitchen or bathroom equipment, you must be mindful that if your supplier lets you down and this has an effect on the progress of the project the builder would have a legitimate claim for extension of time.

- These problems can become even worse if the builder is using a sub-contractor, for example to install your kitchen. If the allocated time is not achieved due to the material not being available, the builder may also have a claim against you to cover the sub-contractor's time lost.

- If you are considering supplying your own kitchen or bathroom equipment it would be advisable to either have them prior to the project starting, or have the builder leave the room ready to receive the equipment.

- Most builders prefer to supply their own material as this is an area where they make a profit on the trade discounts to which they are entitled.

- Your specification should detail the material and it is worth paying close attention to this as some builders may choose to use an alternative that is inferior to that stated in your specification.

Nominated Suppliers & Sub-contractors

- Nominated suppliers and sub-contractors are those appointed by the client and accepted as part of the construction team by the main contractor. The contractor takes full responsibility for the nominated supplier or sub-contractor, although he has the right to refuse instructing them if reasonable grounds exist.

Health & Safety

- It is the responsibility of the builder to work in accordance with the Health and Safety at Work etc Act 1974, and the Management of Health & Safety at Work Regulations 1999.

- These Acts and Regulations are very comprehensive; however, there are basic duties of care that the builder owes to his employees and anyone associated with the project.

- A small building company would normally use a Health and Safety consultant to advise them on the obligations and responsibilities which are to:

    - ♦ Secure the health, safety and welfare of people at work
    - ♦ Protect people other than those at work against risks to their health and safety arising from work activities
    - ♦ Control the keeping and use of explosive or highly flammable or otherwise dangerous substances, and generally prevent people from unlawfully having or using such substances

- If you feel that these obligations are not being adhered to you must bring it to the attention of the builder in order for him to address the problems.

- If the problems continue it is advisable to seek advice from your Local Health and Safety Executive.

'The Design Team'

Project Manager

- On larger projects, where a project manager has been appointed, the client's main involvement would be in the initial concept stages and budgeting details.

  Project management is the effective project control in land, real estate and construction. Project Managers are responsible for controlling or co-ordinating the whole development process.

- Project Managers represent their client to ensure increased efficiency, economy, communication and successful completion of projects based on an original client brief.

Architect/Architectural Technologist

- Specialists in building design and construction techniques. The training for both is similar in many respects, the difference being that architects specialise in concept design issues while technologists specialise in construction and technology. Traditionally appointed as Lead Consultant or Project Leader. Involved from inception through to completion, on larger projects.

Chartered Surveyors

- Chartered Surveyors cover a diverse range of specialist activities dealing with land, property and development i.e Building Surveying, Commercial Property Surveyor, Residential Surveyor, Quantity Surveyor.

Building Surveying

- Building Surveying is one of the widest areas of Practice. Chartered Building Surveyors cover all aspects of property and construction from supervising multi-million pound projects to planning domestic extensions.

- Building Surveyors are experts in investigating problems, diagnosing and remedying defects, and advising on possible con sequences and alternative solutions.

Commercial Property Surveyor

- The work of a Chartered Surveyor in this area covers all types of real estate used for business purposes.

Professional services cover the following:

- Purchase, sale and leasing of real estate
- Management (managing all resources including both human and financial)
- Landlord and Tenant
- Corporate Real Estate
- Telecommunications
- Valuations
- Investment (advice for investment appraisal etc)
- Development and Planning
- Real Estate Finance and Funding

Residential Surveyor

- The work of a Chartered Surveyor in this area covers all types of real estate used for residential purposes. The professional services include:

  - Agency purchase sale and leasing of residential real estate
  - Management of public and private residential property
  - Landlord and Tenant
  - Valuation and Survey of residential property
  - Investment (advice for investment appraisal etc)
  - Development and Planning

Quantity Surveyor

- The Quantity Surveyor may be appointed at an early stage in a project to advise the Client and Design Team of construction costs and procurement methods.

- On larger projects where a Bill of Quantities is required they will undertake measuring and scheduling the building materials to enable the contractors to price accurately.

- They may also prepare tender packages consisting of contracts and documentation. A Quantity Surveyor may provide cost control by way of valuations and certification of payments to the contractor during the construction phase.

Structural Engineer

- A Structural Engineer will advise on structural solutions to building designs. He may advise and calculate the size of structural components and foundations etc. Generally the stability of the structure is his responsibility and he will provide all calculations and details to the Local Authority for approval as necessary.

Environment and other Service Engineers

(Mechanical and Electrical Consultants etc)

- In designing modern structures, many building, environment and other services such as heating and air conditioning need to be considered. The Services Consultant will provide design solutions (layout drawings, specifications etc) to accompany the architectural design and tender packages. Their works may include the following:

    - Plumbing (hot and cold water supplies)
    - Heating
    - Lighting
    - Ventilation (natural and mechanical, air conditioning)
    - Acoustics
    - Sanitation
    - Communications (lifts, escalators etc)
    - Telecommunications
    - Air conditioning

Party Wall Surveyors
(all types of projects)

- Party Wall Surveyors are specialists providing advice and services relating to The Party Wall etc Act 1996.

- The Act provides a framework for preventing and resolving disputes in relation to alterations and extensions near neighbouring buildings.

Facilities Management
(large organisations)

- Facilities Management is the total management of all services to support the core business of an organisation.

- Using 'space planning' the Facilities Manager can implement office relocations of any size and complexity.

- Facilities Managers will look at the best use of space, suitable technology solutions, human resources and safe surroundings.

- Consideration will be given to legal responsibilities such as health and safety, fire protection and escape, access and security.

Planning Supervision

(mainly commercial projects)

- The role of the Planning Supervisor was created under the Construction (Design and Management) Regulations 1994 (CDM) to monitor and improve health and safety issues relating to building, design and construction works.

- These regulations came into effect during 1995 giving the client a statutory responsibility to appoint a competent person in the role of Planning Supervisor, to co-ordinate health and safety matters relating to building projects.

SAMPLE PLANNING PROGRAMME

SAMPLE PROGRAMME

ACTIVITY																	
MONTH	JUNE				JULY					AUGUST				SEPTEMBER			
W/C	3rd	10th	17th	24th	1st	8th	15th	22nd	29th	5th	12th	19th	26th	2nd	9th	16th	23rd
FORMULATE IDEAS AND SKETCHES	■																
CONTACT ARCHITECTS FOR QUOTES		■															
DRAW UP PRELIMINARY DRAWINGS			■	■													
GAIN OUTLINE PLANNING APPROVAL					■												
WAIT FOR PLANNING APPROVAL					■	■	■	■	■	■							
DRAW UP FULL SPECIFICATION						■	■	■									
CONTACT BUILDERS FOR QUOTES								■									
ASSESS QUOTES									■								
NEGOTIATE AND AGREE ON QUOTE										■							
CONFIRM CONTRACT DETAILS											■						
START DATE												■					
COMPLETION DATE																■	
SEND OFF GUARANTEE DOCUMENTS																	■

When you have decided that you are going to undertake any kind of home improvements or major building works, it is advisable to draw up a planning programme.

It is obvious that you will not know exactly the dates on which information etc. will be available, but by having a programme that can be adapted to suit the information as and when it becomes available, you will soon have dates to work to.

As you will see in this example, these are the elements that you need to take into consideration.

SAMPLE SPECIFICATION

Two Storey Rear Extension

Main Building Works

Bricks:	London Stocks, mortar to match existing (sample required)
Blocks:	Lightweight Celcon 100mm thick
Roof Structure:	As per drawing Open cut roof 100 x 50 rafters
Roof Tiles:	To match existing roof Clay 250 x 150
Rainwater Goods:	To match existing, Cast Iron
Windows:	To match existing uPVC double glazed units with lead light effect
Internal Walls:	100 x 50 stud walls @ 400c/c with 12.5mm plaster board & plaster
Heating System:	New boiler and new "period" cast iron radiators, copper piping
Electrical System:	New electrical system throughout as per drawings, faceplates, light switches and light fittings supplied by client.
TV & Phone Sockets:	As per drawing faceplates supplied by client
Carpentry:	Skirting 150mm Torus, Architrave 75mm Torus, Doors and frames, softwood pine six panel to match existing with brass Ironmongery (supplied by client)
Window Sills:	Softwood pine 200mm deep
Wall Finishes:	Three coats white vinyl silk emulsion
Ceiling Finish:	Three coats white matt emulsion
Finish on Bare Wood:	3 coats varnish/stain (sample required)
Kitchen Units:	Magnet Range (see Magnets design & spec sheet) builder to fit only
Wall Tiles:	Fix ceramic tiles with white waterproof grout (tiles supplied by client)
Floor Finishes:	Lay stone floor tiles in kitchen (supplied by client)
Carpets:	Client to arrange supply and fit
Curtain Rails:	Fix 100 x 25 pine backboard for fixing curtain poles
External Work:	Lay 1m wide paving slabs around external walls of house where indicated on drawing, to specification indicated on main drawing

SAMPLE PROGRAMME OF WORKS

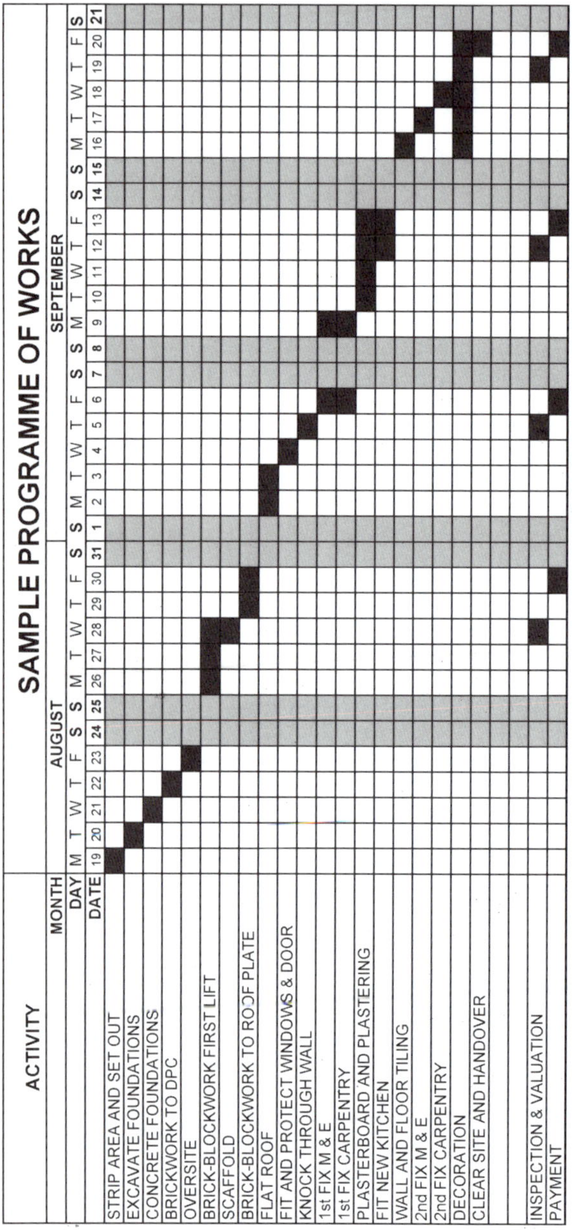

As you can see from this example, there is a sequence of work that will apply to all types of home improvements or major building works.

It is important to have such a programme in order to measure the works against the time specified for it.

You can also incorporate in your copy of the programme the dates for inspections and payments.

SAMPLE CONTRACT OF AGREEMENT

Client Name: ________________________________
Address: ____
____

We agree to employ the services of [BUILDER'S NAME] to carry out our building works all in accordance with the drawings, programme and specification herewith and as per agreed quotation in the sum of £_______

Client signature: ________________________________
Date: ____

....

Builder's Name: ______________________________
Address: ____
____

We agree to carry out building works for [CLIENT'S NAME] all in accordance with drawings, programme, specification and as per our quotation in the sum of £________

Builder's Signature: ________________ Date: ________________

Specific conditions to contract (circle) YES NO

Bonus payment for early completion of project £________ per week

Other conditions: ____

Documents forming part of this contract:

• Drawings	YES	NO
• Specification	YES	NO
• Sketches	YES	NO
• Quote	YES	NO
• Insurance Details	YES	NO

Third Party Signature: ____________________
Print Name: ____________________
Date: ____________________

ONE COPY TO CLIENT----------------ONE COPY TO BUILDER

SAMPLE METHOD STATEMENT

Name of Contractor:	CIRCULATION: Client Architect Surveyor Other

Date:	Job No:	M.S. No:

Site Address:

Details of work:

Location of work:

Plant to be used:

Method to be adopted:

Safety precautions to be taken:

Prepared by: Position:

FURTHER READING

The Housebuilder's Bible
An Insider's Guide to the Construction Jungle
Written by Mark Brinkley
Ovolo Publishing Ltd
Telephone No: 01487 824704

CONTACTS FOR FURTHER INFORMATION

Blackberry Books	01983 840310	www.blackberry-books.co.uk
Building Bookshop	0207 692 4040	www.buildingcentre .co.uk
Build It	0207 772 8300	www.insidecom.co.uk
Homebuilding and Renovating	01527 834406	www.homebuilding.co.uk
Building Your Own Home	01909 591652	www.selfbuild.armor.co.uk
Selfbuild & Design	01283 742970	www.selfbuildanddesign.com

To order JCT Building contract for home owner/occupier
Building Bookshop 0207 692 4040

Health and Safety issues/advice
HSE Infoline 08701 545500

INDEX

A

B

C

D

E

F

G

H

I

J

L

M

N

O

P

Q

R

S

T

V

W